23 TIPS TO
LEARN
STUFF
BETTER

so you can spend less time studying
and more time enjoying yourself

Ian Gibbs

23 Tips to Learn Stuff Better
© 2018, Guid Publications

Bruc, 107, 5-2
08009 Barcelona
Spain

Email: guid@guid-publications.com

Cover design: Ian Gibbs
Interior design: Estudio Hache

ISBN:
978-84-948660-2-9 paperback
978-84-948660-3-6 ebook

www.guid-publications.com

This book is dedicated to my wonderful children,
Alex and Sol.
May your curiosity and enthusiasm never wane.

"I really enjoyed this book. It's very easy to read and it's written in a very simple, funny and accessible way. I think it's fantastic for all teenagers who are studying. And also I think this book should be read by teachers, because it gives ideas about teaching as well as giving ideas about how to learn stuff better. I think this book will help me a lot in my next high school year. I recommend this book to all teenagers and to all teachers who teach teenagers."

\- Martina Capallera Sais (15 years old)

CONTENT

With Pen and Paper

With a little help from your friends

Over and Out

INTRODUCTION

When I was 18, I said goodbye to my family and travelled 300 miles to St. Andrews in Scotland to start life as a university student studying astrophysics. At that time for me, there were two types of students: those that went to wild parties and got average grades and those who studied hard and got good grades. I had it really clear: I wanted the best grade I could get. So for four years, I said no to the wild parties (most of the time) and studied as hard as I could. It was tough, but when I finished university, I left with a grade that was absolutely… average. Oh well, that's life, as they say, or so I thought.

Fast forward 30 years. Same student, less hair, more stomach. This time, the subject was Catalan. I needed to learn it, and fast. So I decided to do some research. I consulted the websites of language learning gurus such as Benny Lewis and Matthew Youlden. I was pleased to discover lots of language learning techniques. And they were really useful. They help me a lot. But what I started to realise was that these language learning techniques weren't language learning techniques. They were simply learning techniques and could be used to learn anything. And that's when I had my epiphany: Learning is a skill. Just like you can learn to read or write, you can learn to learn, too.

At first I felt really pleased about this, and then I felt quite upset. Why had nobody told me this when I was a student? It might have come in really useful!

Back in those days, I thought the best way of studying was reading books and making notes for long, late-night sessions that lasted until the early hours of the following morning.

Did you know that's one of the least effective studying techniques there is?

If someone had told me how to learn twice as much in half the time and remember it for ten times longer, I could have got the grades I wanted and gone to the parties. I could have saved myself thousands of hours, had a great social life and left university with the degree I wanted, which would have meant I could have had the pick of the top jobs and started earning good money straight away.

It didn't happen to me, but it could happen to you. It's not too late. It's all about knowing the right things and having the right attitude. So let's start by considering the following three statements and whether you agree with them.

- You need a high IQ to learn something well.
- You need a great teacher to learn something well.
- You need to study really hard to learn something well.

If you agree, you might be surprised to discover they are all false. A high IQ, a great teacher and lots of hard study undoubtably help, but none of them are necessities.

Regardless of our IQ, we can all learn things. For example, we've all learnt to speak at least one language fluently. In fact, most people in the world are fluent in at least two languages or more and they're no cleverer than you.

Without having a teacher, you've probably learnt an impressive amount of stuff already. Think about the long list of names and details of all the people you know: your family and friends, not to mention your sports heroes, your favourite actors, your most worshipped pop-stars and most-liked social media celebrities.

And you learnt it without any 'hard' studying at all.

In fact, the biggest factor regarding your ability to learn is how good your learning technique is, or in other words, the way you go about trying to do it.

Getting an education is tough. Trying to get through the academic year with those dreaded exams looming on the horizon can be stressful and frustrating. Especially if no one's explained to you what the best ways to study are. But asking students to learn difficult subjects without showing them how to learn is like asking someone to fly a jumbo jet without teaching them how to be a pilot. It's a disaster waiting to happen.

So, as I don't much care for disasters, neither aeronautical nor academic, that's the objective of this little book: To show you how to learn stuff better.

In this book, you'll find 23 tips to help you study. If you can put them into practice, you'll find learning becomes easier. You'll start to become a capable learner. You'll get better grades, better results. You'll have a better chance of successfully getting the job you want, or being accepted by the college or university you want. And as you continue, you'll start to develop confidence regarding your studies. You'll enjoy them more. You'll leave behind everyone else who doesn't understand there are better ways to learn stuff.

You can go from being a below-average student to an above-average student. You can go from being an above-average student to a top student. You can go from being someone who tries, to someone who succeeds. Furthermore, you'll have the choice of passing on this knowledge to your classmates, your friends and eventually even to your own kids.

Can you imagine that? Can you imagine how relieved you'd feel to get better grades, to pass instead of fail? Can you imagine how proud you'd be to show your report to your family? Can you imagine being able to leave school to get the job you want or get into the college or university you want because you got the grades you needed? Can you imagine earning more money because you got better results?

It doesn't have to be something you just imagine. You can turn your dream into a reality.

This book will help you achieve that.

It's not cheating. It's not illegal. It doesn't involve breaking any rules. These tips can help you learn a new skill or new knowledge in a way that will impress.

Simply put, this book can help you become a superhero of studying.

I hope you enjoy it.

HOW TO USE THIS BOOK

On these pages are what I believe to be the most useful tips on how you can learn stuff better. There are others (see 'What's Not in This Book' at the back for further details). The ones I have included here, for me at least, are the most practical, the ones that are the easiest to apply and that will serve you best.

Nevertheless, I encourage you, the reader, to think about your own experiences. Maybe from somewhere in your past you can remember a few learning tricks or techniques that would work for you. You knew them once but they sort of got pushed to the back of the cupboard and forgotten. By all means, bring them out, dust them off and add them to this book on the pages especially reserved at the back.

The last page is there to allow you to reflect on the twenty-three tips and to evaluate yourself. Which of them are you strong in already and which still have room for improvement?By the way, this book is aimed at teenagers. This is because if anyone could benefit by improving their learning skills it is the stressed teenager, under more pressure than ever to learn stuff for their GCSEs, A-levels or for their college or university degree.

However, if you don't happen to be a teenager, please don't be put off. I know for a fact that the content of this book continues to help my adult students (as well as myself) just as much as the younger generation.

Finally, given its usefulness, I don't recommend just reading this book and then putting it on a shelf to gather dust. I'd much sooner suggest keeping it on your desk, bedside table or wherever it is you do your studying so it can serve as a constant reminder and be there to 'dip into' every once in a while to help you keep your learning skills as sharp as you can.

I wish you all the best putting these tips into effect. Learning can be a wonderful adventure but only if you set off carrying the right equipment. I sincerely hope these learning tools help make your learning adventure as rewarding and successful as possible.

If you want, you could skip the next few pages and get stuck in but if you prefer to get your money's worth, why not start and consider your current learning skills by doing a little quiz?

QUIZ

1) If you're finding it difficult to learn something, what do you usually do?
   a) Leave it and go on to the next thing to learn.
   b) Copy from a friend.
   c) Get help.

2) When you are told to do something in class, you usually…
   a) do what you're told.
   b) do it if you feel like it.
   c) do it by thinking, 'how could I do it better?'

3) When learning a new topic, you usually…
   a) just try to remember your teacher's explanation.
   b) look for more explanations on the internet.
   c) reread the coursebook.

4) How often do you ask your teacher about what you'll be covering next lesson?
   a) Always.
   b) Occasionally.
   c) Never.

5) When do you do your homework?
   a) As soon as possible.
   b) As late as possible.
   c) The dog ate it.

6) When it's study time, you usually…
   a) study in one long session to really get as much done as possible.
   b) study in several short sessions.
   c) put it off until tomorrow or perhaps the day after or maybe next week.

7) You usually study…
   a) somewhere quiet.
   b) wherever you happen to be.
   c) anywhere that makes you feel like studying.

8) What usually breaks your concentration?
   a) Unplanned interruptions.
   b) Distractions.
   c) Boredom, hunger or bodily functions.
   d) Your alarm reminding you to take a break.

9) In your opinion, mistakes are usually a sign that you are…
   a) stupid.
   b) tired.
   c) learning.

10) When you make a mistake, you usually…
   a) ignore it and focus on what you do know.
   b) make a flashcard of what you need so you don't slip up again.
   c) feel bad and promise yourself to try harder next time.

11) Do you have your homework sessions programmed in your agenda or study timetable?
   a) Yes.
   b) No.
   c) What's a study timetable?

12) You usually do your homework…
   a) at different times in the same places.
   b) at the same times in the same places.
   c) at the same times in different places.
   d) at different times in different places.

13) The last time I used some sort of reward or punishment to help motivate me to study was...
    a) This week
    b) Last month
    c) Last year
    d) None of the above

14) You usually use flashcards...
    a) a few weeks before the final exam.
    b) from the very start of the year.
    c) I don't use flashcards.

15) When you read a coursebook, you usually...
    a) read it several times.
    b) underline the key points.
    c) fall asleep.

16) When someone tells you something important, you usually...
    a) say thank you.
    b) think 'That's important. I must try to remember it'.
    c) write it down.

17) Looking back through your notes, most of the illustrations are...
    a) doodles.
    b) childish illustrations of your teacher.
    c) there to help you understand and remember.

18) You usually give an explanation of what you've learnt...
    a) when someone asks you to.
    b) as a regular part of your study routine.
    c) when trying to impress people at parties.

19) You ……….. work with a study buddy.
   a) always
   b) often
   c) occasionally
   d) never

20) The last time you made a game out of what you were studying was…
   a) within one week.
   b) within one year.
   c) at nursery school.

21) If you find something difficult to learn, you usually take it as a sign that…
   a) you're stupid.
   b) you need to think about it more.
   c) your teacher didn't explain it well enough.

22) When you've more or less got the idea of something, you usually…
   a) move on to the next thing to learn.
   b) practise it even more till it's easy.
   c) celebrate.

23) At bedtime, if you ask yourself 'What did I do today?' it's because you…
   a) are reflecting on the day's events.
   b) are trying to go to sleep.
   c) want to learn stuff better.

Q1: a=0, b=0, c=2 Q2: a=1, b=0, c=2 Q3: a=0, b=1, c=2 Q4: a=2, b=1, c=0 Q5: a=2, b=1, c=0 Q6: a=1, b=2, c=0 Q7: a=1, b=0, c=3 Q8: a=0, b=0, c=0, d=2 Q9: a=0, b=0, c=2 Q10: a=0, b=2, c=0 Q11: a=2, b=0, c=0 Q12: a=1, b=2, c=1, d=0 Q13: a=2, b=1, c=0, d=0 Q14: a=1, b=2, c=0 Q15: a=1, b=2, c=0 Q16: a=0, b=1, c=2 Q17: a=0, b=0, c=2 Q18: a=0, b=2, c=0 Q19: a=1, b=2, c=1, d=0 Q20: a=2, b=1, c=0 Q21: a=0, b=2, c=0 Q22: a=0, b=2, c=1 Q23: a=0, b=0, c=2

Score:

0 to 15: You probably don't enjoy studying much. You find it frustrating. Hopefully, by applying some of the tips in this book you can start to change that, if you want to.

15 to 30: Your studying skills are normal. But there's still a lot you could be doing to make things better for yourself.

31 to 40: Well done! You're a good student but could still improve your technique a bit further.

41+: Congratulations! You're clearly an expert on how to learn stuff better. Pass this book on to someone who needs it more than you.

23 TIPS TO
LEARN
STUFF
BETTER

THE BASICS

1: OWN IT

I used to have a classmate who could have won the Olympics at inventing excuses. Every single problem he had was somebody else's fault. If he got up late, he complained it was his mum's fault for not waking him. If he got to class late, he moaned about the bus driver and the traffic. If he failed his test, it was the teacher's fault for not teaching him properly.

These excuses might be acceptable from a child, but not a student. Whether you like it or not, it should be you in control of your life. You are the one. You can accept this responsibility or you can give it away to someone else. But if you give it away, don't get upset when that person doesn't accept it or doesn't use it the way you want them to.

If it's important to get up early, then own it. Set your alarm clock (or two) and make sure you get enough sleep.

If you need to arrive on time, own it. Don't leave it till the very last minute to set off. Unexpected delays happen. You know this.

And what about your studies? If it's not going well, you can blame your teacher or your parents or the government or your dog. But by doing that you're saying you aren't able to do something about it yourself. Maybe that's how you've felt up until now. But the truth is you're the only one who can learn what you need to. No one can learn stuff for you.

A cook can prepare food to make it as appetising as possible, but whether you eat it or not is up to you. And if you were ravenous, you wouldn't need a cook. You'd be perfectly capable of raiding the fridge all by yourself, wouldn't you?

Learning stuff is just the same. If you want to, you can learn with or without your teacher's support. You are perfectly capable. After all, think about all the stuff you've learnt without the help of a teacher.[1]

Whether it's playing your favourite computer game or using your smartphone, I doubt you had a teacher who stood over you and told you what to do. You figured it out for yourself, or you found someone else who could help you and learnt from them.

And so it is with the stuff you study. You can complain that your teacher doesn't explain things the way you want or the coursebook is boring or the subject is difficult and then get all indignant when you fail your exams six months later. Or you can take matters into your own hands and do something about it.

You might feel this isn't fair. Many times I've heard "but my teachers get paid and I don't. They're the ones who should

---

1- Such as interacting socially, learning the lyrics of songs and negotiating with your parents to get what you want make more effort". If you want to think like that, fine. Go ahead. But as far as your education is concerned, it's not going to improve anything and, quite frankly, it's a bit pathetic.

Could you imagine James Bond doing his training? Imagine he didn't get on with his Russian teacher. Can you imagine him in the canteen of MI5 moaning, "This is so unfair. My Russian teacher is stupid. I hate him. I'm never going to be able to speak Russian. It's all his fault. Sniff, sniff"? No. He'd own the situation. He'd take the initiative and do something about it.[2] He'd find a way to learn with or without his teacher.

Whether you like it or not, the responsibility of your education is yours. Own it.

By owning your education, you can start to improve the situation right now. You can start to change things. You can change the way you study so that it fits your needs. You can change how you do your homework to get it done better. You can change the way you get on with your teacher so it's less stressful. You can change it so that by the time you leave school, you'll have learnt something useful. And possibly the most useful thing you can learn is how to learn stuff better. That way, whatever you want to learn in the future, you'll be able to learn it the best you can.

So please, do yourself a favour. Own it.

When you find yourself struggling with your studies, ask yourself this question: 'What can I do to improve things myself?'

2- Which would have nothing to do with shooting anyone.

It might seem difficult. It might feel strange. But you have a choice: you can improve the situation and learn the stuff you need or you can ignore things, pretend some magic pixie[3] is going to come and save you at the last minute and then act all surprised when you don't get the grades you want.

Tip 1: Take responsibility for your learning. If you're not doing as well as you'd like, do something about it.

3- For many, this magic pixie is called 'cramming' or intense studying the week before your exams, desperately hoping that you'll be able to understand in a week all the stuff you haven't been able to understand in a year. I'm sorry to disappoint you, but the magic pixie won't be coming to save you.

2: DON'T DO WHAT YOU'RE TOLD

Washing machines are great, aren't they? You choose the temperature, duration and spin speed and, all being well, that's what your washing machine does.

Your toaster works in a similar way. You choose a setting between warm and burnt and that's what you get.

One day, I hope to have a robot that when instructed will clean the kitchen, take the dog for a walk and bring me a full English breakfast in bed with a copy of the morning news. That would be lovely.

But, as you know, you're not a robot. You can think for yourself. You're not limited by what someone (your teacher) tells you. Although flatly refusing to cooperate will only cause problems, there's absolutely no reason why you can't do more.

'Do more?' you exclaim. Before you start wondering what sort of idiotic book this is, please let me explain.

When your teacher tells you what to do (for instance, when setting homework), she sees the situation from her position: a teacher talking to a class of students of various abilities.

But you see it from yours. You know your strengths and weaknesses. You know if the task is hard or easy.

If it's hard, then maybe rereading a few pages from your coursebook (even though you weren't told to do so) might be a good idea. In this case, the extra reading would make the task easier (and quicker) to do. So you invest time and effort at the beginning to save it (and get a better result) at the end.

If it's easy, then by simply doing minimum, you're not going to learn much more and your teacher won't see how much you know either. So perhaps by doing a little bit more (such as adding a diagram or a few interesting factoids), you'll learn a bit more and give the teacher reason to give you a better grade come assessment time.

Whether you call it thinking for yourself, taking initiative or being proactive, it's an important ability you should develop. It's not only useful for learning stuff better, it's also important for impressing future employers or running your own business. So start thinking for yourself, think 'out of the box' every time you are given an assignment.

For example, you've been asked to write a 500-word review of a film you've recently seen. Your teacher has suggested you break it up into an introduction, body and summary. But if you thought for a moment, you might decide to divide the body into 'best bits', 'worse bits' and 'surprises'. Or, if you prefer, 'characters', 'conflicts' and 'resolutions'. Whatever you use is going to make the task clearer, more structured and easier to do which means doing it in less time and getting higher marks.

So the next time your teacher explains an activity or sets you homework, take a moment to think and ask yourself these questions:

- ✓ What is the objective of this task?
- ✓ What hasn't my teacher said that might be useful?
- ✓ How could I do the task better?

By taking a few moments to think and do something you're not specifically told to do, you can avoid problems, save time/effort and do the task better.

Don't sit around waiting to get spoon-fed—you're not at primary school anymore. Think for yourself and start making things happen so you can start learning stuff better.

Tip 2: Don't wait to be told what to do. Start thinking for yourself.

3: GET IT YOURSELF

Back in the dark ages, your teacher would have been the only source of knowledge you had. If you were lucky, there might have been a coursebook as well that you could read in class. If you were really, really lucky, you'd have been allowed access to the school library, if you felt like it, which you probably wouldn't have, because it was dark, dusty and smelt funny.

In the dark ages, knowledge was in short supply and getting your hands on it was difficult, costly and time-consuming.

But now things are very different. Getting access to knowledge, in user-friendly packages, has never been easier.

If it's something you need to know for your school work, there are probably a dozen websites already waiting for you to visit.

If you prefer the moving picture (and, let's face it, who doesn't?) there'll be several YouTube channels dedicated to explaining just what you need.

And if you prefer something more interactive, there's probably an app for that, too. There are apps for learning chemistry, spelling, maths and geography. There are apps to learn French, German or even Esperanto. There are even apps to help you organise your homework.

And many of them are totally free!

An excellent way to start is to check out 'Khan Academy' (webpage or app), 'Crash Course' or 'TED ed' on YouTube. They provide beautifully clear explanations you can watch as many times as you like without annoying anyone.

The point is you no longer have to struggle remembering the explanation your teacher gave in class. If you didn't get it the first time, there's a myriad of material on the World Wide Web whose sole purpose is to help you learn whatever you want.

Maybe you didn't understand something you did in class.

Maybe you want to understand a bit better.

Maybe there's something you missed in class because you were absent or because you were dreamily contemplating the cloud formations out of the window.

The reason is not important. What is important is you can now search for knowledge in ways that were impossible just a few years ago.

So wouldn't it be nice to turn up to the next class having completely understood the previous one?

Wouldn't it be great to have just as good a grasp of your subject as everyone else in class? Or an even better grasp?

Wouldn't it be amazing, when your teacher points to you and asks you to explain what the last lesson was about, you could stand up and confidently do it without fear or hesitation?

Finding the right 3-minute explanation and watching it enough times for you to get it can help you achieve all of the above by using the internet to learn stuff better.

Tip 3: Find out the answer to your questions yourself. Save time and effort by using the internet to your advantage.

BONUS TIP 1:
WHATEVER YOU LIKE

If you're interested in chemistry or geography or English literature, then good for you. Enjoying the subjects you have to learn is a big help.

But what about if the things you're interested in aren't on your school syllabus? What if the thing that interests you the most is horse-riding or drone-piloting or playing in a band or setting up your own restaurant?

The answer is simple. Learn as much as you can about whatever it is that does interest you.

You might say, 'but what's the point if it's not part of your school's studies?'

Regardless of what you learn, you'll start learning stuff your fellow classmates don't know.

If you continue learning, after a while you'll discover you've become an expert compared to the rest of your class. If you continue further, you'll become an expert in your year. A little further still and you'll be the expert in the whole school.

This means when you leave school, regardless of your grades, you'll be an expert in your subject.

Think about that for a moment.

If you know how to do things most others don't, then getting a job or offering your services is much easier because you can do stuff others can't. In business they call it 'competitive advantage'. What it means is you can do stuff better than anyone else.

Another reason to learn extracurricular stuff is that, although it might seem extracurricular to you, it probably ties in with stuff that is on your curriculum.

You can't do much with drones without picking up stuff about drag, lift, friction, energy and radio waves, and that's just physics.

Horse-riding involves biology, including anatomy, biochemistry, nutrition, as well as animal psychology, logistics and business skills.

Playing in a band involves the mathematics of music, the physics of acoustics and amplification, as well as teamwork, negotiation skills and marketing.

Running your own restaurant involves finance, customer psychology, advertising, interior design, etc. etc. etc.

At some point, the stuff you learn about your own interests is going to overlap with the subjects you learn at school. And when it does… click! It will satisfyingly snap into place. You'll find it easier to learn because you've learned half of it already.

What's more, a useful tool for learning is the use of metaphor. A metaphor is when you compare something to something else in order to understand it better (e.g. the flow of water is often used as a metaphor to describe how electricity behaves). If you have learnt lots of stuff, you'll have had lots of experiences others haven't. When you need to understand a new concept, you might be able to use the stuff you've already learnt as metaphors for the new.

And even if the stuff you learn doesn't appear on the syllabus and doesn't help you find work, it still makes you a knowledgeable and more interesting person. You never know, it might not be useful today, but tomorrow… who knows?

Bonus tip: Learn about anything that interests you, even if it's not on the curriculum at the moment, it'll probably come in useful later on.

IT'S ABOUT TIME

4: DARE TO PREPARE

If you've ever been to a concert, I bet the songs you enjoyed the most were the songs you already knew.

In fact, I also bet you even made an effort to listen to those songs before going to the concert. It feels perfectly natural, doesn't it?

But why? Why make an effort to go somewhere to listen to something you've already heard?

The reason is because you need time to absorb new stuff. You need time to mentally process it, to digest it, to take it in.

Listening to the music before the concert helps you familiarise yourself with what you're going to experience. You will be a little more relaxed about the event. You can enjoy it more.

Exactly the same thing applies to the topics you cover in class. If you can familiarise yourself with the topic of a lesson before the lesson, you'll be able to mentally process it better.

How do you find out what you'll be doing next lesson?

If you're following a coursebook, just skip forward a few pages (but be careful, your teacher might not be covering every chapter). If you're not following a coursebook, try asking. The fact you're showing interest in the lessons is usually enough for your teacher to let you know what's coming next.

Once you've found out what the next lesson is about, use your skills at searching the web to find something that will explain it to you before the lesson.

By taking a few minutes to go over what you're going to be doing before the class, you'll get it quicker, so you can spend less time having to concentrate and more time pretending that this is sooo easy and that you're sooo intelligent.

It means that even with the usual classroom distractions of gossip, humour and rivalry, you can still come out on top and look cool.

So find out what the next lesson is about, do some research before the class and discover for yourself how a bit of preparation helps you learn stuff better.

Tip 4: Find out what's coming up in the next class and do a bit of research to be one step ahead of everyone else.

5: THE SOONER, THE BETTER

If you pick up a soaking-wet towel, the water drains from it quickly at first. But then after a while, the draining water slows to a steady drip, drip, drip until the rest of the moisture in the towel dries by evaporation.

Your memory works in a similar way. Immediately after a lesson, the amount of stuff you need to remember from that lesson quickly starts draining away. The longer you leave it, what little information you can still remember continues to disappear until you can hardly remember anything at all.

What this means is if you want to be as efficient as possible, if you want to learn the maximum amount with minimum effort, you have to act as quickly as you can after a lesson.

This is a dilemma. On the one hand, you want to get out of class and start getting on with something more interesting as soon as possible. But on the other hand, if you want to spend the least time and effort remembering the stuff you need in

21

order to do your homework, you must strike while the iron is hot. You need to do it while it's still fresh in your mind.

One way to achieve this is to jot down a few of the key ideas from the lesson to outline your assigned task as soon as you can.

For example, at the end of the lesson, your teacher explains the homework while everyone is stuffing their bags and trying to get out the door all at the same time. If you take just thirty seconds to write down the main points from the lesson and sketch out what ideas you have for doing your assignment, when the times comes to actually doing it, you'll find these notes a useful reminder and a huge help.

So set down key ideas or underline the most important points which you'll need to include right at the end of class.

Similarly, it's much better to do homework sooner than later.

Let's admit it. It's tempting to do homework as late as possible, the night before (or even the same morning) it has to be handed in.

By doing it as late as possible, you're making sure you've forgotten as much as possible. This means you have to waste time and effort trying to remember stuff you would've easily been able to remember a week earlier.

So if you know you're going to have to do your homework anyway, why not do it on the same day it was set? You'll do it quicker, better and get a higher grade for less effort. Wouldn't that be great?

And how would you feel going the whole week knowing your homework was already done (and done well) while everyone else was struggling and stressing themselves trying to remember what it was they were supposed to have learnt?

It would just be another sign that you're the one who knows how to learn stuff better.

Tip 5: Don't leave things till the last minute. Take a couple of minutes to jot down instructions and key ideas for doing homework immediately after class and then do the homework the same day.

6: DO A LITTLE OFTEN

In 2003, most of Europe suffered a drought. The temperatures were blisteringly high and the rainfall was pitifully low. The following year saw heavy rainfalls, but this didn't solve the drought. Instead of the rainwater going into the ground and hydrating the dry earth, it just poured across the top, flooding large areas and eventually running off into the sea.

This happens because the ground needs time to absorb rainfall. It can't absorb water instantly. It absorbs much more if the rain falls little and often.

Your brain works in the same way. I'm sure you might have already found this out for yourself. If you try to learn lots of stuff in one huge study session, come the next day, you can hardly remember any of it.

Doing a little often is much better than trying to binge and do a major learning task in one go. Doing five 20-minute sessions of homework (a total of one hour and forty minutes) is much more productive than one 4-hour session. After the first half-hour of concentration, your brain starts to get tired. It becomes harder to remember stuff and think clearly.

Studying for shorter amounts of time guarantees your mind is fresh and responsive.

By doing just 20 minutes of homework whenever you can, you'll be making sure you're not wasting your time by trying to learn too much stuff in one go.

You'll be surprised at how much you can do at lunchtime or break time if you can find a quiet place to work.

The same thing goes for revising: You can learn more stuff from six 10-minute sessions than one 60-minute session.

By applying this technique of doing a little often, you'll be able to remember more things and spend less time trying to do it. So while your friends are staying in, doing all their homework late into the evening and getting average grades, you can relax knowing you've already learnt more, and with less time and effort.

That definitely means you're learning stuff better.

Tip 6: Learn more by studying for shorter periods more often.

IT'S MENTAL

7: FIND YOUR SPACE

Have you ever had to go to the swimming pool on a blustery winter's day? You probably didn't feel like going swimming at all. Outside, it was cold, wet and windy. Staying at home (or even at school) where it was warm, dry and cosy seemed so much more preferable to going out.

But once you got through the horrible weather and through the doors of the local swimming pool, something changed. The smell of chlorine, the sound of nearby splashing and echoey laughter and that incredibly hot and humid air was just begging you to get out of your winter woollies and into your swimwear. Swimming didn't seem like a good idea before you arrived, but now you're here in the changing room, it seems like the only logical thing to do. Your attitude has changed and all because of your surroundings.

Do you realise how much we are influenced by our surroundings? Shops, restaurants and cinemas all design their spaces in such a way to get us to do what they want (buy more stuff than we intended). The sights, the sounds and the smells all combine to get you to want to put your hand in your pocket.

This is the power our environment has. And the same thing goes for studying.

Our attitude to studying is affected by where we are.

Because of this, it's a really good idea to study in a suitable place each day. Libraries are great for this—they're quiet and with few distractions. The knowledge stored in all those books almost radiates from the shelves. Usually there are others there who have come to study, too. Just like swimming felt natural at the local pool, studying feels like the natural thing to do at the library.

But if you don't do libraries, anywhere reasonably free of distractions can be good, too.

The best thing is to have a regular study centre: the usual place where you work. The more time you spend there learning stuff, the more natural it will feel the next time you sit down there to do your homework.

Even if you don't feel much like studying, just like at the swimming pool, once you're sat down surrounded by your books, paper, computer, pens, Tippex, pencils, rubber, highlighters, lucky study-mascot and whatever else you usually need, you'll start to feel that learning something is the only natural thing to do.

One thing you can do to help your environment help you to study is to get yourself a 'study lamp'. A 'study lamp' is just a normal table lamp or angle-poise lamp. Perhaps you've got one already. But the trick is to only turn it on when you study. You can even label it 'My Study Lamp'. If the lamp is on, it's time to learn something. If the lamp is off, it's time to do something else. It's a visual prompt to get you in the right frame of mind.

So start paying attention to what places and features help you get into the right mood for studying and use them to your advantage. By adapting to them, you'll find yourself slipping into study mode more naturally and with less effort, which means you're doing it better.

Tip 7: Study in a place that helps you feel like studying.

8: DEEP THOUGHT

Have you ever been scuba diving? There's lots of fascinating stuff at the bottom of the sea but it's not easy to get to. You have to do a lot of preparation and then swim down further and further, slowly moving through the layers of water until you get to where you want to be.

In this way, thinking is similar to scuba diving. If you want to consider all the points of a difficult essay or solve a tricky problem or practise a particularly challenging manoeuvre, you need to focus your thoughts as much as possible.

If you want to learn stuff better, you need to concentrate.

As a diver, if you had to keep coming up to the surface to say hello to a friend, read a text message or get something to drink, you'd hardly spend any time at the depth where you wanted to be.

Similarly, if you're constantly being interrupted or distracted, you won't be able to delve down into the inner recesses of your mind to get the important bits of your brain doing what you want them to do.

Do yourself a favour and avoid interruptions. Go somewhere where you won't be disturbed, put a sign on the door or simply ask your family not to interrupt your study.

Get rid of as many distractions as possible. This includes the TV, the radio, etc. It means putting your phone on flight mode and closing down your social media. If you find this a challenge, there are apps designed precisely for this purpose. Look up productivity apps such as 'Freedom' or 'StayFocused'. These apps either block or limit the amount of time you spend on potentially distracting sites such as Instagram or Facebook.

Think seriously about turning off your music, too. If you have to listen to music, best listen to music without words. You might think it doesn't matter but there's part of your brain that pays attention to lyrics. If it is paying attention to lyrics, it can't help you do your homework if your homework involves thinking in words. This is partly why some experts recommend a nice bit of Chopin or Mozart as classical music doesn't have words. This isn't so important if your task is drawing, sculpting, dancing or playing any type of sport. But if you're writing, reading, listening or speaking, I'd recommend you stay away from music with lyrics.

Maybe you've heard this sort of thing before and think it doesn't apply to you. Maybe you're convinced you're an expert multitasker. You know, the sort of person who can read, watch TV, text and have dinner all at the same time. Unfortunately, it's normal to think like this. This is because it's difficult to realise how inefficiently you're doing something when you're in the middle of it.

Test after test after test shows how we fail to notice stuff, or make unnecessary mistakes, or do stuff more slowly or fail to remember stuff when we multitask.

When you're multitasking, you're superficially engaged most of the time and constantly backtracking to find where you were when you flipped your attention from one task to another.

What doesn't help, either, is it takes mental energy to keep shifting your attention. This means your brain gets tired much quicker.

This is another reason why it's better to concentrate only on studying for just a short period of time of, say, half an hour. Then take a break and eat, text, whatever in between. In fact, even if you don't have anything else to do, it's recommended you get up, stretch and do a bit of exercise. It gets the heart pumping, which gets more oxygen to the brain.

With deep thinking, it's definitely quality rather than quantity that counts. An hour of shallow thinking is not as good as half an hour of deep concentration.

So do yourself a favour and practise improving your power of concentration by focussing on your task and ONLY on that task for thirty minutes.

Just like the scuba diver, if you stay deep down in your thoughts, you'll find those important ideas and connections you need to get the task done quicker. This means you'll be able to complete your work sooner and have it done better, while all the multitaskers are still taking twice as long to produce stuff that's only half as good.

Tip 8: Save time and work better: concentrate more.

9: MAKE MISTAKES

Making a mistake is a bad thing, isn't it?

Yes… and no. It depends.

If you're a brain surgeon or a Jumbo Jet pilot or a nuclear scientist, then yes—a mistake can most definitely be a bad thing.

But if you're a student, making a mistake isn't so bad. If you're learning something new, it's normal. It's to be expected. It's all part of the process.

Go to the ice rink and watch a figure skater practise. See how many times he falls down. Go to a studio and watch an actor in rehearsals. See how often she forgets her lines. Go to the circus and watch a pair of jugglers trying to learn a new set. Count how many times they drop their juggling balls again and again and again. Anybody who's trying to learn anything makes a mess of it, and often.

You learn something by trying to do something difficult. When you try to do something you can't do, you make a mess of it, whether it's trying to juggle, do long multiplication, speak a new language or write a prize-winning essay.

Getting it wrong doesn't mean you're stupid. Getting it wrong shows you're trying to do something that for the moment is beyond your capabilities and that's great because that's how you stretch yourself. That's how you learn.

If you're worried about making mistakes, it's going to cause you stress. It'll stop you from trying new things and stretching yourself.

Rather than trying to avoid making mistakes at all costs, accept them as part of the process. Don't worry, be happy that you're progressing through the learning process.

If you accept that making mistakes is okay, you can relax a little. You'll find it easier to start. You'll find it easier to explore. You'll find it easier to learn and you might even enjoy it a little more.

While your classmates are still waiting, unsure of what to do to get a perfect result, you'll have already started, if not finished. You get much more out of an activity if you start than if you just stare at a blank screen or a blank sheet of paper for half an hour.

So the next time you get it wrong, don't deduce that you're hopeless. You tried, and that's a good thing. Keep at it. Keep making mistakes. Sooner or later, things will start clicking into place.

Tip 9: Don't feel bad about making mistakes; accept them— it's an important part of the learning process.

10: LEARN FROM YOUR MISTAKES

Having said that making mistakes is good, I think we both know that if you keep making a pig's ear out of your subject every time you try, something isn't as it should.

If you're trying to do a chemistry experiment that keeps exploding, something somewhere is going wrong. If you're trying to ask someone in French for a glass of water and they just don't understand you, there's a problem.

The whole point of making mistakes is to learn from them. What went wrong? What caused the mistake? What weren't you doing right? What could you do differently next time?

If you simply repeat the same action only to get the same result, you're not learning, you're just acting stupid.

When you make a mistake, pay attention to it. Don't grimace and try to ignore it or cover it up. Look at it and say to yourself, "That's interesting. Why did that happen?" Identify the reason. Maybe it's because you forgot an important step. Maybe you confused one thing with another. Maybe you simply haven't practised enough. Maybe you're mentally exhausted and need a rest.

The Wright brothers, who invented the aeroplane, made lots of mistakes. They had hundreds of crashes. But each time, they made the effort to learn from their mistake. They adapted. They improved. They worked on the problem and their success is history.

The same goes for whether you're trying to build a spaceship to Mars, understand Shakespeare or do a Sudoku.

It doesn't matter what the reason for the mistake is. What matters is that you pay attention to why it happened and learn from it.

Once you've identified the problem, you can focus on it and try to make sure it doesn't happen again. Make a note of it. Make a flashcard of it. Make a picture of it and stick it somewhere you'll frequently see it. Practise just that bit a few dozen times. Repeat it correctly till it sinks in. But whatever you do, don't ignore it. That's not learning. Ignoring your mistakes is just you trying to fool yourself.

Learning from your mistakes doesn't mean getting everything right the next time. You're allowed to keep on being occasionally wrong. If you got five out of ten on your last exam, then getting six out of ten is still an improvement, isn't it?

Mistakes are there to let you know what you still need to practise. Pay attention to them. They are not your enemy. They are friends helping you to learn stuff better.

Tip 10: When you make a mistake, don't ignore it. Identify what the problem was and learn from it.

BONUS TIP 2:
DON'T DO THIS

In Tip 9 we looked at not worrying about making mistakes.

In Tip 10 we looked at learning from the mistakes we do make.

But in this Bonus Tip (which, to be honest, is really more of a Warning than a Tip), we're going to look at a big mistake which you definitely should worry about making and from which there is almost nothing to be learnt at all.

In fact, this mistake is so big and so bad it's one of the main reasons why students like you don't get the grades they could.

Avoiding this mistake can improve your grades not just by 1 or 2% but by 10 or 20% or more.

The mistake is this: Believing that the stuff you can RECOGNISE is the stuff you can RECALL.

Let me explain.

Knowing stuff by recognition is the simplest kind of knowledge there is. For most of us, recognition is easy. You're probably very good at it. For example, you should be able to look at hundreds of photos, each one for just a second, and yet still recognise any that are repeated. You easily recognise what you've already seen.

But just because you've already seen something in a book or already heard your teacher talk about something in class, that doesn't mean you're going to be able to remember (recall) it the next time you need it. It's not the same.

I used to make this mistake all the time. I'd leaf through my notes, thinking 'Yeah, yeah, yeah. I know that... and that... and that.' Yet when the end-of-the-month test arrived, or even worse, the end-of-year exam, suddenly the simplest of things I was sure I 'knew' had mysteriously vanished from my head!

Surprise, surprise!

Being able to recognise something is not the same as being able to recall it from our memory whenever we want.

And even though you're reading this thinking 'This is obvious. I don't make this mistake', I bet if you went back and reread the previous chapters in this book, you'd probably think 'Yes. I've got it.' But if, instead, you had to make a list of the tips you've read so far without looking, you'd struggle to remember half of them.

The only way to tell the difference between recognition and recollection is to do it. Test yourself frequently. Try to remember stuff just before you open your textbook, not just after you've closed it.

If possible, get someone else to test you. Or write down your own questions today and try to answer them tomorrow. Make flashcards (more about these in Tip 14).

But whatever you do, don't confuse recognition for recollection. Recollection is necessary for the next level of learning which is understanding[4] (or comprehension, as it's sometimes called). That's when you start to get it. You start to see how all the different things you're learning fit together and interact with each other. But it's difficult to understand things like the Maastricht Treaty if you can't even recall where, when or why it was signed.

So do yourself a favour and increase your grades by remembering that recognition and recollection are two different things and one should never be confused for the other.

Bonus Tip 2: Learn to tell the difference between stuff you can recognise and stuff you can recall.

4- If you're interested in a quick explanation of the levels of learning, see the short appendix at the end of this book.

GETTING STARTED

11: PLANNING

When you were at primary, your time was very much decided by your teachers at school and your parents at home.

But as you start thinking for yourself, you start to take more responsibility for your own wellbeing. You start to decide when would be the best time to do stuff—even the stuff you don't feel like doing.

Planning, or if you prefer, the-ability-to-do-something-today-that'll-make-your-life-better-tomorrow, is one of the most important skills you can develop. After all, if we all went about doing whatever we felt like doing whenever we felt like doing it, our lives would be a complete mess, wouldn't they?

Maybe you already know someone who is a bit like that?

But why? Why is planning supposedly so important? What's the problem with doing stuff when you feel like doing it?

The problem is called distraction.

For instance, if you have a choice of two activities where one is your not-so-much-fun history homework and the other is listening to your friends tell you about why Harry and Sally got detention in their Biology class, the latter is probably more interesting at that moment. It grabs your attention.

And your life is full of attention grabbers: friends, gossip, rivals, text messages, romantic interests, social media, after-school activities, important announcements. And when you get home there's the fridge, the TV, the internet, parents, more social media, siblings, more messages, etc., etc., etc....

In short, there will always be something more interesting, more 'shiny', than studying.

But not necessarily more important.

If you postpone the important things every time you find something shiny, you'll never get round to doing any of them.

This is a problem.

As we've already seen, the longer we delay doing an assignment, the more we'll have forgotten from the previous lesson.

Planning is a way of reminding yourself to stop the shiny stuff from getting in the way of the important stuff. It's a way of helping yourself focus your attention on those important things.

If you like, you can draw up a study timetable or modify your school timetable to include homework sessions.

If your weeks tend to be too irregular for a timetable, then another option is to use a homework app. These allow you to plan out your assignments and they send you reminders when necessary, which is very helpful.

A simpler solution is just to set yourself a study alarm or reminder which basically says 'Stop whatever you're doing and start studying now'.

Whatever system you come up with, a bit of forward planning will help you get your homework done sooner, better and with higher grades. Planning helps you avoid forgetting, procrastinating or being distracted by the shiny stuff.

It will help you effectively get through that steady flow of assignments, making sure it never builds up into an unconquerable mass and avoid those feelings of stress and frustration.

By planning your time, you can get through more stuff per day and make sure that when it comes to going out for the evening to those truly important social events, there won't be any problem because all your homework will have already been done.

Tip 11: Plan your study sessions in advance and don't let the shiny stuff distract you.

12: THE POWER OF HABIT

We are all creatures of habit, and this includes you, too.

By this I mean that you tend to do the same thing in the same way every time you do it. Just think about it:

The way you fold your arms.
The way you hold your pen.
The way you sit in class.
The way you eat your food.
The way you go to bed.

Did you know that stuff you do regularly is handled by a different part of your brain? You don't 'think' about doing it; it becomes 'instinctive'—part of your mental hard-drive. In other words, you do it automatically.

What this means is that the more you do something, the more natural it is to do it. And it's a really good idea to bear this in mind when it comes to learning stuff.

If you're not used to doing the things we've looked at so far (such as finding a good place to study, making notes at the end of class or doing assignments on the same day as you're given them), then the first few times you do them will feel strange. It will feel unnatural because you're not used to it. You're used to doing things the old way (remember, the old way was when you struggled to learn stuff well).

But the more you apply these ideas like finding help on YouTube, preparing for lessons in advance, and planning your study sessions, then the easier and more natural it will feel.

On your very first day when you travelled to school, you probably felt a bit weird, a bit uncomfortable. Maybe you even felt a bit nervous. But now, you've probably done the journey so many times, you do it every day without giving it a second thought.

Studying is exactly the same. If you start doing it differently, it will feel strange at first, but if you keep at it for a few weeks it becomes easier and easier until learning stuff better becomes the natural thing to do.

Tip 12: Carry out the other tips in this book regularly. It becomes much easier to do them if you do them often.

13: TRICK OR TREAT?

I'm sure you're already very familiar with prizes and punishments at school—especially the punishments.

But the reason why your teachers dish them out is because they can be terribly effective when used in the right way.

The only problem is you probably have your doubts about whether they really are being used in the right way.

After all, you are the best person to decide whether a prize or punishment is going to really help you do what you should be doing, aren't you?

You know exactly what those little things are you enjoy or hate. You know exactly what works with you and what doesn't.

So here's another question to think about: The next time you should be sitting down to study but you don't really feel like it, what can you do to help get yourself motivated?

What prize or punishment could you use?

Examples of what other students use are...

- ✓ Thinking of how relieved you'll feel once you've done it
- ✓ Giving yourself a chocolate when it's finished
- ✓ Promising your mum you'll do the dishes/empty the bin/hoover the house if you don't do your homework
- ✓ Not using social media until it's done
- ✓ Thinking of the satisfaction that getting it out of the way will produce
- ✓ Thinking of the pain/embarrassment/stress that not doing it will produce
- ✓ Not doing your favourite activity until it's done
- ✓ Giving yourself a homework point for doing it[5]
- ✓ Celebrating with your favourite drink and your favourite food while listening to your favourite music
- ✓ Get your dad to hide your phone until your assignment is done
- ✓ Get your family to give you a round of applause for finishing it

The reward (or punishment) doesn't have to be big, it just needs to be big enough to work. It doesn't even have to be for finishing. It could be a reward for sitting down and starting.

5- I know a few people who have created their own points system. They award themselves a point for doing whatever-it-is-they-want-to-do. They collect them, adding them up day by day. When they get to a certain number of points (10, 50, 2000), they reward themselves by treating themselves to a luxury bath, a favourite meal or a new farmhouse in France.

Simply listening to your favourite music (without lyrics, remember?) while you study is one example of this. I like to sit down and start studying with a nice cup of tea, but that's just me.

In Tip 7, you read about the importance of studying in the right place. If it is 'rewarding' just to sit down there, all the better. If it feels comfy, good. If the background noise is pleasant, fine. Even the right smell can influence your attitude. These little details are all little rewards in themselves.

So the next time you're struggling to start your study session, try using one of your own prizes or punishments to help you sit down and get started.

If you can make this into a regular habit, you should find getting started becomes easier and your grades start steadily rising.

With better grades comes more confidence, more self-esteem and a better feeling about yourself altogether. And that's one of the best rewards there is, isn't it?

Tip 13: Use a prize or punishment to help increase your motivation.

WITH PEN AND PAPER

14: DON'T LOSE THOSE NUGGETS

You probably already know what flashcards are: small rectangular cards with the stuff you want to learn written on the back and some sort of question or prompt written on the front. You go through each card looking at one side and trying to remember what's on the other before turning it over to see if you were right.

If you've ever prepared for an exam, you might have already tried using them.

But here's the important bit: If you combine flashcards with Tip 5 (The Sooner, The Better), Tip 6 (Do A Little Often) and Tip 12 (The Power of Habit) you can create one of the most powerful ways to learn anything you want.

Don't wait until exam time to make flashcards. Start making them from day one. Not hundreds of them, just one or two for each lesson.

Go to your local stationery shop and invest in a pack of blank cards. They usually come in packs of a hundred.[6] Take a few blank cards to school and, during class, try to identify what the key points are. What are the nuggets of knowledge your teacher is trying to teach? Write them (preferably in pencil) each on a card and then take them home and keep them next to the place you study. If you already have a blank card handy, making a flashcard only takes a few seconds.

Over the weeks, your pile of flashcards will steadily grow. In fact, if you're keeping track of your nuggets, you'll need to go back to the stationer's before Christmas.

Of course, making your own flashcards is only half of it. The other half is to regularly go through them to see what you can remember. And when I say 'regularly', I mean 'every day'. Not necessarily looking at all of them. But a few—at least the top ten cards or as many as you feel like.

The power of this method is that the steady trickle of information going through your mind keeps what you've learnt fresh and firmly in place.

While your classmates have already forgotten what you did a few weeks ago, you'll have it clear in your mind. You won't have to worry if your teacher gives you a test out of the blue, you've already learnt it.

6- You can even get them bound on a big ring to keep them together but those are more expensive. Personally I prefer them loose, as they're much more flexible to work with. Save your money on the ring-bound type and use a rubber band instead.

And by the time you get close to your exams, you'll impress yourself by how much you've learnt and how easy revision is.

Flashcards are a simple and convenient way of remembering nuggets of knowledge.[7] They can also be used in different ways to help you learn.

- ✓ You can get the pack and go through them one by one as you lie in bed.
- ✓ You can set them out face down on the table and select the ones you choose to revise.
- ✓ You can divide them into groups: Easy, Okay and Difficult and spend more time revising the difficult ones.
- ✓ You can challenge yourself to how many you can get right without making a mistake.
- ✓ You can compete with a friend and turn it into a game.
- ✓ You can get someone to test you with them.

Another advantage of flashcards is you can count them. This might sound trivial, but there is something very satisfying about seeing all your cards together and realising just how much you've learnt so far. If you can say 'I've learnt 147 things so far this term', it gives you a nice feeling of progress.

And one final recommendation: When you go through your cards, if you're able to, write down your answer BEFORE you turn the card over. It's tempting to try to convince yourself you knew the answer all along. But there's a big difference

---

7- It's only fair to point out there exist a variety of flashcard apps that you might like to investigate. They are good. In certain circumstances, I recommend them. But for learning a variety of subjects, most students find real cards more versatile.

between recognition and recollection and only one of these is going to get you through your exams. So don't fool yourself—jot down your answer before you flip the card over. That way you can really prove to yourself that you are learning stuff better.

Tip 14: Flashcards are one of the best ways of remembering stuff that's important. Start your flashcard collection from day one.

15: SOMETHING TO DO WITH A PENCIL

Maybe you already know this game, but an entertaining way to pass the time on a long journey is to play 'Things you can do with...'. It helps develop your creativity and can be very funny depending on who you play it with. The idea is simple. Someone thinks of an everyday object such as a paperclip, a ping-pong ball or a house-brick. Then you take it in turns to think up different uses for the aforementioned item. For example, if the chosen item were a 'pencil', then possible uses could be 'stabbing a hole through a piece of plastic, 'as an axle for a homemade toy car' or 'to remove something unpleasant from the bottom of your shoe'.

But one use of a pencil you mustn't forget if you want to learn stuff better is to <u>underline key bits of text while you're reading</u>.

Be honest: How many times have you found yourself halfway through a page of your coursebook only to realise you have no idea what it is you've just read? This happens because, although your eyes were on the page, you were thinking about something else.

Following what you're reading with the tip of a pencil serves as a <u>visual guide</u> and <u>helps you pay attention</u> to the task.

Gently underlining the key points helps you mentally engage. It <u>makes you think about what you're reading</u> instead of thinking about something else.

Having paid more attention and underlined the key points means you won't have to waste time rereading the text. You just need to skim over it, quickly returning to the important bits. This <u>makes summarising much simpler</u>.

And finally, once you've gone through your text and want to make a few <u>flashcards,</u> it's much <u>easier to pick out</u> the key <u>nuggets</u> if they're already underlined.

But don't get overenthusiastic. <u>Don't underline too much</u>. I've seen books where almost entire pages have been underlined. This is counterproductive. If all the words are underlined, then none of them are going to stand out.

What about if what you're reading is on the <u>computer</u>?

You have a choice.

Either <u>print it off</u> and work with it on paper <u>or</u> copy and <u>paste it into a document</u>. This way you can underline using the computer or use the highlight facility.

In fact, I know people who prefer to highlight their texts instead of underlining in pencil. If you prefer highlighting, fine. The main difference is that if you change your mind, <u>you can't rub out highlighter</u>, so you're stuck with it whether you like it or not. Pencil is forgiving. It lets you change your mind whenever you want.

Without this simple technique, it's more likely your concentration will stray. You'll lose track of what you're reading and have to waste your valuable time and effort going over it again. Without having underlined bits, when you get to the end you won't have identified the key points and so won't have such a clear idea of what to do next.

Notice how <u>the underlined text in this tip helps</u> draw your attention to the main ideas.

In short, it <u>saves you time</u> and <u>gives your thoughts structure</u> to easily build on—a simple but effective way of helping you learn stuff better.

Tip 15: When studying a text, <u>underline the key points in pencil</u>.

16: ASSUME YOU'LL FORGET

There's a man called David Allen. Lots of people think he's a productivity guru—a man who knows how to get things done.

But when asked his secret, his answer was "Get something called a 'pen' and get something called a 'piece of paper'... and write stuff down."

You need to write stuff down so you don't have to remember it (at least not at first).

Your brain didn't evolve to remember stuff like names and dates and numbers. It evolved to figure things out like how to find food and how to avoid becoming it.

If you write stuff down, no matter how simple, it helps you remember the next time you come back to it.

We've already seen the importance of underlining key points when reading from a text. But what if there's no text to underline?

For example: this morning, your teacher gave you a few really good ideas to help do your homework. Brilliant! But that was hours ago and by 7pm you find yourself sitting in front of your exercise book struggling to remember even one of them.

So often we trip over the same stone time and time again. We think we're going to remember, but we forget. The time between hearing (or thinking) an important idea and needing it is filled with distractions, interruptions and temptations. Remembering is a futile task.

Please, do yourself a favour. Assume you're going to forget.

Imagine, at a raucous party, someone you really like tells you their number and asks you to call them tomorrow. Wouldn't your first reaction be to make a note of the number?

Treat every important idea as you would a potential date's phone number.

When your teacher gives you a couple of suggestions for how to do your homework, write them down.

When you come up with your own great lyrics for a song on your way to class, write them down.

When you overhear someone say something worth remembering about a chapter, a lesson or a subject, write it down.

At that very moment when it's there fresh in your head, it'll seem so clear, so obvious, so evident, that making a note of it is just insulting your intelligence. But the real insult is when you get round to setting pen to paper (or fingers to keyboard) to do your task and realise the memory has become vague or, even worse, has completely vanished.

Write it down. Write it down clearly using enough words to make sense. If not, you'll find yourself staring at the page wondering what on earth 'calp th hzedl' was supposed to mean?

Jot down your ideas in the margin or at the back of your exercise book. Use an app on your phone. Write on the back of your hand. Leave yourself a voice message. Carry round a little notebook and pen. Take a photo. Whatever you do, if you assume you'll have forgotten by the time you need the idea, you'll be right more often than not.

And of course, do it immediately. Because two minutes later, something else will catch your attention and that important idea, that key concept will be lost, buried under a pile of other not-so-important things that urgently need your attention.

If you do this, every nugget of information that passes your way will be trapped for you to examine and use whenever you want.

You won't have to struggle trying to remember because you'll have it fixed down already. While you're not worrying about trying to remember messages and instructions and explanations, you can confidently focus on the juicier bits of gossip and school scandal that requires your undivided attention.

Tip 16: Assume you'll forget and write down your important ideas.

17: PICTURE THIS

Remember those children's story books you had read to you when you were little? You know, the ones with all the pictures. Have you ever thought why they had pictures in them?

It's because we find pictures much easier to understand. We remember them better than words, too.

You might read about Romeo and Juliet, or The Battle of Hastings, or how to make hydrochloric acid, but if you could see a picture, you'd start to understand better. After all, that's why most textbooks have diagrams and photos, isn't it?

But when it comes to learning, it's even better if the picture was created by you. You might not be the world's best artist— it really doesn't matter. There are lots of different ways of making pictures. Even little stick-people riding what look like giant potatoes with legs and smiley faces might be fine under the right circumstances.

If you're writing an essay on the pros and cons of recycling, you could support it by creating a diagram to visualise the arguments for and arguments against. You can draw them or copy and paste them. It doesn't matter. You don't even have to include the diagram if you think your teacher won't approve.

But regardless of whether your teacher sees it or not, come exam time you'll find it much easier to remember the picture you made representing your studies and so find it easier to answer the questions.

So add more diagrams to support your work. You could illustrate your French homework with example drawings of new vocabulary or comic-style people with French speech-bubbles.

Make them colourful. Make them stand out. Use humour. Use your imagination. The more creative your picture is, the easier it will be to remember.

In fact, why be satisfied with two dimensions, when you could make a 3D model? Get hold of some coloured plasticine and make a model of your internal organs. Get your box of Lego from out of the cupboard and build a model of the European Union. What was the point of learning how to make stuff out of papier-mâché if you can't use it for creating your own model of a courtroom or the periodic table?

Creating stuff you can visualise is a powerful technique to remember stuff. While your classmates are struggling to come up with all the different sources of renewable energy, you'll be able to close your eyes and visualise all of them because of the cartoon you drew with the funny captions and rude bits nobody else gets to see.

Tip 17: Learn better by anchoring ideas using images.

WITH A LITTLE HELP FROM YOUR FRIENDS

18: EXPLAIN IT TO SOMEONE ELSE

A teacher once did an experiment with two groups of students. She gave the same homework to both groups. But there was one difference. She told the first group there would be a test the following week. She told the second group they would 'just' have to explain what they had learnt to the rest of the class.

The following week both groups were given the same test. The first group straight away. The second group did the test but only after each person had explained what they'd learnt, not to the whole class but just to a fellow student. And which group did best in the test? The second one, those who had explained it beforehand.

When you explain something to someone, you use different parts of your brain than you would if you just thought about it silently. When you talk about a subject, you process your thoughts in more ways and you remember them better.

If you can, when you study, explain what you're doing to someone else. If you don't have a study buddy (see next tip), tell your mum or dad (they might even be interested in hearing about what you're studying), or talk to your granny, your big sister, your little brother or the dog. Even if it's just talking to the poster of your pop idol or sports-hero on the wall, it will help.

Talk to them as if they were a student in your class. Don't just tell them about what you're studying. Teach it to them. Explain it to them as if they knew nothing about it.

When you do this, you put your ideas in order, understand them better and remember them more.

So the next time you're trying the learn something challenging or complicated, try teaching it to someone else and you'll find that you'll be teaching yourself at the same time.

Tip 18: You learn better when you teach it to someone else.

19: TWO HEADS ARE BETTER THAN ONE

You've just seen in the previous tip that if you explain something to someone else, it helps you understand it better.

You could even go one better and get a study buddy.

For most of my time at secondary school, I struggled with my subjects. I did my homework on my own, sat at the dining room table. It wasn't exactly something I 'enjoyed'. But that changed when I teamed up with Gary. This happened when we started our 'A' levels. Gary was the only other person doing all the same subjects as me. So it was quite natural that we drifted together, but I'm very pleased we did.

Having a study partner made all the difference. It made it much more interesting and enjoyable. Discussing the stuff we covered in class and the assignments set for homework helped both of us understand better. We did some work together and at other times spoke by phone about problems we had. Putting our ideas into words helped us connect one concept to another and remember better.

Just like it sounds, a study buddy is a friend who's studying the same stuff you are. The key thing is you study together and help each other.

This doesn't mean one of you does the homework for the other.

What it does mean is you talk about what you're studying, share ideas and help each other. It's not cheating. It's a way of learning that works.

Other kids will go home and struggle in silence. They won't get the benefit of another's point of view. They won't consolidate their ideas by talking about it. They won't be reminded of that really useful hint their teacher gave while they were distracted.

If you can arrange to sometimes do your homework with a study buddy, you'll find you start to 'get it'. You'll have more 'Ah ha!' moments. Ideas will start to click into place.

But one word of caution: be careful to stay on track. It's easy for a conversation about learning stuff to turn into gossip and banter. To avoid this, here are a few recommendations:

- ✓ Set yourselves a clear objective.
- ✓ Set yourselves a time limit.
- ✓ Agree not to stray off target.
- ✓ Help each other to do it for yourselves.

And one final recommendation: Don't worry if one of you is doing better than the other. This will almost always be the case. If a stronger student helps a weaker student, the stronger student also benefits from the interaction. It's a win-win situation. But only if it's genuine help. If the weaker student is just allowing the stronger student to do everything, that's not really helping at all.

The best way of working together is to work alone for the first part and then to compare notes, discuss points and share ideas afterwards. This gives both of you a chance to think for yourselves before consulting with your partner. Don't get too dependent on each other. Study separately, too. Tackling problems by yourself is also important to do sometimes. But get together regularly, enough for it to become a useful routine.

So why not make the effort? Try doing your homework once or twice a week with a friend. In fact, you could even go one better and set up a homework club where a few of you get together. It can turn homework into a social event. If it was good enough for Harry, Ron and Hermione, it's good enough for you.

Tip 19: Nowhere does it say you have to do it alone. Get ahead, get a study buddy or two.

20: JEUX SANS FRONTIERS

Why is it so easy to spend a few hours playing Call of Duty, Minecraft or Pokemon and yet so difficult to grind out thirty minutes of trigonometry or crop-rotation farming? Or is this just a stupid question?

I'm sure you're already well aware that playing games with the stuff you study makes it a bit more interesting. So when was the last time you used this to your advantage? When was the last time you played a game that helped you learn stuff better?

If your answer was something along the lines of "It was when my teacher told me to", then you're probably not making the most of this learning technique.

Playing with knowledge helps you relax a bit. It helps your mind open up a little more and so helps you remember stuff better. Just because your teacher hasn't told you to do so is no reason to miss out on the opportunity. You can play games to help you learn better whenever you want.

What games?

Broadly speaking, there are three types: Pre-made games, Study Buddy games and On-Your-Own games.

Pre-made games are all the games that have been created for the sole purpose of helping you learn. We're talking about apps and websites like Kahoot! or Quizlet. Pick your subject, do a search and you'll find someone, somewhere, has created a game to help you learn. The only problem with them is that because they are made for the general public, the questions are general, too. The chance of you getting a pre-made game to help you with precisely the stuff you were doing in class today is slim.

Study Buddy games are things you can play with your partner. Their advantage is you can easily focus them on the stuff you're studying right now. Of course, much depends on your partner's creativity and enthusiasm. If you're stuck for ideas, try these.

- ✓ Test from the coursebook. One of you gets to play the teacher with the book, asking the questions. The other gets to play the poor student trying to prove they've understood and remembered the important bits.

- ✓ Talk for two minutes on a theme. One of you gets to choose a topic and control the timer. The other gets to talk for the agreed time without hesitation, repetition or straying off the subject.

- ✓ True or false. A simple but effective way of quizzing each other on the subject and at least a 50% chance of getting it right.

✓ Flashcards. There's lots you can do with flashcards, but if your creative juices have dried up, just testing each other from your own or each other's flashcard pack can be satisfying.

If you're having a study session with a friend or two, why not arrange to round it off with a 10-minute game? It's nice to change the dynamics of a study session. Whereas most of a study session is spent reading, discussing, explaining, comparing ideas and answering questions together, doing something which is more likely to produce laughter and a bit of friendly, creative banter can produce a welcome change of mentality, which after an intense bout of concentration, might be just what you need.

The final type is 'On-Your-Own' games, those you can play by yourself. This is hopefully where all the flashcards you've been collecting over the weeks come in handy.

We looked at a few different ways of using flashcards to learn stuff better in Tip 14. To make this a little more challenging, why not compete against the clock? How many cards can you get right in five minutes? How long does it take to get twenty right? Keep a record of your score. That way, you'll have a realistic target to beat next time as well as the satisfaction (when you do beat it) of seeing for yourself that you're making real progress.

To summarise, whether you compete against the computer, your study buddy or just against yourself, playing with your newly-learnt ideas is an effective way of getting them to stick in your head better and for longer.

Add a learning game or two to your learning toolbox and use it often. It might be just what you need to learn stuff better.

Tip 20: Playing games with the stuff you're learning allows you to relax a little, adds variety and helps you remember stuff for longer.

OVER AND OUT

21: DO IT AGAIN

There's a guy on YouTube called Mike Boyd. Look him up. He's great. He learns stuff. Not German or Geography but fun stuff like axe-throwing or dice-stacking or spinning a basketball on one finger.

But the reason why I recommend him isn't just to watch the fun stuff he does. It's also to look at how he does it.

You see, most of us approach learning new stuff with a bit of uncertainty: "Dice-stacking? What's that? I'm not sure if I'd be very good at doing that."

You have a go and, of course, you inevitably fail.

You have another go, and another, and another. And, of course, you fail, fail and fail again.

By the time you get to the tenth or twentieth attempt (assuming you've managed to get that far), you're probably saying to yourself, "This is really difficult, too difficult for me. Look how badly I'm doing. I'm no good at this at all. Nope, I'm definitely rubbish at it. Yup, that's me—rubbish at dice-stacking. I think I'll give up now before I waste any more time."

Take 'dice-stacking' and replace it with 'French' or 'algebra' or 'archery'. That's how it usually goes, isn't it?

Think of something you're 'rubbish' at. You only need to have a couple of goes at it to prove just how bad you are.

But let's go back to Mike.

When he sets himself a new thing to learn, he's just as rubbish at it as you or me. He starts his new project on 'Day one, hour zero' and records himself. He videos himself trying to do it but doing it badly, failing, time and time again. He doesn't just fail ten times or twenty, but fifty, a hundred, two hundred, five hundred.

For example, look at his video of him learning how to spin a basketball on one finger for over 30 seconds. Eventually (and after a lot of video-editing) he manages it after practising for a total of 4 hours and 39 minutes. That's right, 4 hours, 39 minutes to go from can't-do to can-do. With an average of 10 seconds per attempt, that's more than 1,600 fails.

I'll repeat that. More than one thousand six hundred fails.

Don't be put off if you don't get something the first time, or the fiftieth time. If you want to learn something, you need to practise it, time and time again.

Fortunately, most things you're studying don't need to be repeated 1,600 times to learn them. But the number is still higher than you probably think.

So don't give up too easily. Just because you didn't get it on the first or tenth attempt, doesn't mean you can't. You have to keep trying. Keep learning. Keep going until the 'click' comes.

For anyone learning something new, there is a 'click' or an 'Ooooo' moment.

The 'Ooooo' moment is when there's a breakthrough—something happens and your progress makes a sudden leap. There's a moment when it all starts to come together. Something becomes noticeably easier.

These moments are important. They are signs that your brain is starting to learn, clicking bits of knowledge and experience together like bits of Lego.

Once you've had one click, another click will come along quicker than the first one did. Breakthroughs will start happening until what you're studying starts to feel easy.

You can get to that point, too. You can study something difficult for a long time. But at some point—click. Suddenly, finally, amazingly, you start to get it.

If you're struggling with something, set aside an hour at the weekend and keep at it. Whether it's irregular verbs, quadratic equations or perfecting your backflip, countless others with lesser abilities than you have managed it and if they were able to do it, so can you.

Tip 21: Trying and failing repeatedly is a natural and necessary part of learning something new. Don't let it put you off.

22: OVERLEARNING

As well as writing books, I also help people learn how to speak in public. It's an important skill. Giving a presentation to a large audience in a clear and appealing way is not something most people find easy.

Often, if someone has to prepare a speech, they write down what they want to say and then practise it until they can remember the words without looking at their notes. That's as far as they go.

But this is a mistake.

The mistake is to stop practising once you are able to remember.

Why?

Because if you do this, when the time comes to give your speech you'll find yourself in front of your audience struggling to remember your words, looking worried and feeling like a fool.

This happens because when you give a presentation, you get nervous. Being nervous makes it more difficult to remember stuff. You find yourself struggling. This makes you even more nervous. It gets even worse when you realise the stuff you could (just) remember during practice has now mysteriously disappeared from your mind.

It's a common problem. It happens to everyone who has to talk in public. It also happens during exams. You're sitting at your desk, absolutely certain you knew enough to answer the questions last week. But now… it's gone.

The way to avoid this situation is to do what I get my students to do: keep practising even though you can remember it. By doing this, you ingrain what you need to learn. It becomes second nature. You don't have to think about it, you just do it. With my public speaking students, I get them to continue practising, until they get to the point where they can give their talk while washing the dishes, cleaning their teeth or making a sandwich.

This process is called overlearning. It's continuing to study stuff you more-or-less already know until you REALLY know it. You know it so well, you can do it without thinking, without making an effort, without struggling or getting stressed.

For average students, it's normal to be in the middle of a test only to discover that what they thought they knew has vanished.

Avoid this by overlearning. Once you think you understand, go over it again. Rewatch the explanation on YouTube. Do a few more exercises. Redo the same exercises. Explain the whole thing again to your study buddy.

Whatever you do, allow the stuff you're learning to really seep in and become fixed. This way, when you are in the stressful situation of really needing to remember what you've learnt, there won't be a problem. When the teacher has asked you a question and all the class is staring at you, you'll be able to answer calmly and concisely. When it's exam time and you've only got a few minutes left, you'll be able to produce the goods without a moment of hesitation.

Overlearning is the way to make sure that the stuff you know when you're relaxed and have plenty of time stays learnt when you're stressed and in a hurry. That's when you can tell that you've been learning stuff better.

Tip 22: Don't stop when you've more-or-less got it. Keep practising till it becomes automatic.

23: WHAT DID YOU DO TODAY?

One of the most annoying questions you get asked when you get home from school is "What did you do today?"

Answering this question requires a lot of complicated memory retrieval, the shuffling around of ideas and thought vocalisation. Let's be honest, when you get home, what you need is a bit of chill-out time, not third-degree interrogation.

So let's change the subject for a moment.

We earlier looked at how learning stuff little by little is much better than trying to cram it in all in one go. So here to end with is one little-by-little tip to do at the end of each day that will help a lot.

Once you're in bed with the light off about to go to sleep, ask yourself this question: What did I learn today? Think back to each class you had. What did you do in each lesson? Can you remember? What was the point of each lesson? What were the nuggets of knowledge from each one? What flashcard(s) did you make? What was the homework? What did you do to learn stuff better?

There are a few reasons why you might like to get into the habit of doing this each night.

1: Summarising your memories of the day's studies helps you understand. It's like explaining your thoughts to someone else, only in this case the 'someone else' is you.

2: Having these thoughts just before you go to sleep helps you transfer them to your long-term memory. In other words, it helps you remember them for longer. When you wake up, your subconscious mind will have been processing those thoughts, storing them in a way that's easier to retrieve them. This means when you want to remember them, they'll be easier to find.

And if that's not enough, thinking about what you've learnt today is a great way to make yourself fall asleep. Getting enough sleep is very important for learning stuff better. If you're not getting enough sleep, your thoughts become 'fuzzy' and your ability to remember stuff plummets.

The best way to learn is little by little, by doing something, anything, every day. And every day includes today.

So when you turn off the light tonight, ask yourself 'What did I do today?'. If the answer is 'nothing', then you're not doing yourself any favours.

Going over at least one nugget of knowledge might seem trivial, but over the days, weeks, months, the nuggets will build up into something truly impressive.

Two and a half thousand years ago, a little old Chinese fellow called Confucius said, "If you want to move a mountain, you have to begin by carrying away small stones".

The mountain you're moving is all the stuff out there you need to put inside your head. By doing it one nugget at a time every day, slowly but surely those nuggets will start to stick together to form your own little mountain of knowledge that will continue to get bigger and bigger.

While everyone else drifts off to sleep thinking about almost anything else apart from what they've been studying, you'll be consolidating your day's studying, helping yourself to understand it better and remember it for longer.

This means that come next class, you'll have a stronger foundation of understanding, so the next lot of nuggets will have something solid to rest on.

It also means that when it comes round to exam time, you'll have a much, much easier time of things because you'll have already been doing your own mini bedtime revision all year. So preparing for exams won't cause you half as much stress as it's causing everyone else. You'll be able to confidently finish the year knowing you've already learnt your stuff to the best you can.

Tip 23: Just before you go to sleep, ask yourself 'What did I learn today?'

24: THAT TINY BIT EXTRA

The difference between ordinary and extraordinary is that little bit extra. So here's a final tip my father taught me when I was at school: Do a little bit extra.

If your homework is to read a chapter, read a chapter and the first page of the next.

If your task is to answer 10 questions, answer 11 (if there isn't an eleventh question, make one up).

If there isn't anything obvious you can do, consider doing one of the following:

- ✓ Illustrate your work with a diagram.Evaluate your own work: What are its strengths and weaknesses? How could it be better next time?
- ✓ Take a few minutes to search YouTube for more ideas/ information.
- ✓ Write a note explaining what you got out of the homework.

In short, do what you're asked to do and then do a little more.

Your work will stand out because it has something extra. Your teacher will notice and will have reason to increase your assessment grade. Your teacher's attitude towards you might even improve, too.

These small extra bits start to add up and accumulate. Slowly, you start progressing that little bit better than the average person in your class. You will start to feel comfortable with the pace of lessons instead of struggling to keep up.

As my father said, 'You don't have to be much better to be better than the rest'. All it takes is putting in that little bit extra.

Extra tip: Do what you have to and then do a little extra.

WHAT'S NOT IN THIS BOOK

You've just read my own 23 tips to learn stuff better. I hope they serve you well. But this doesn't mean that's all there is. There are other points which didn't make it into my list that you might like to think about. Just because it's not so important to me, doesn't mean it won't be important to you.

Consider the following and if you'd like to learn more, I've included a recommended read.

Sleep

Getting enough sleep is not only important for learning stuff, it's also important for living a healthy life in general. I haven't included it here as, in my experience, it's easier to get penguins to juggle melons than it is to get students to go to bed early. If you are interested in learning more, I suggest reading 'Why We Sleep' by Matthew Walker.

Exercise

Getting regular exercise is also important for getting the little grey cells to work better. They need oxygen and when the heart is pounding away, oxygen (carried in the blood) is supplied to the brain in larger doses. I haven't included it here as, since most students rely on public transport, they already get a fair amount of exercise. If you are interested in learning more, I suggest reading 'Spark!' by Dr. John J. Ratey.

Memory Tricks

There are hundreds of different ways to remember stuff. They are all useful. I haven't included them here because, although they are good for remembering things, they're not much help with being able to understand and evaluate things. Furthermore, to do them justice you'd need a whole book dedicated just to them, such as 'How to Remember (Almost) Anything' by Rob Eastaway.

Diet

If I had a pound for every time I heard about how our diet affects our thinking, I'd be able to keep the dog well fed for a month. The funny thing is that even though I know all about it, I still eat the same rubbish. I haven't included diet here because if I did I'd be branded a hypocrite for the rest of my life by anyone who knows me. If you are interested in learning more, I suggest reading 'The Care and Feeding of Your Brain' by Kenneth Guiffre and Theresa Foy DiGeronimo.

Attitude

Having the right mental attitude towards doing anything (not just learning stuff) is, of course, important as well. But I haven't included it here because it's not a 'tip', it's a whole outlook on life. Giving a tip along the lines of 'Have a positive attitude to learning' is like saying 'Cheer up' to someone who's suffering depression. It's just not that simple. Nevertheless, if you want to learn more, I recommend 'Mindset' by Carol Dweck.

Theory

The way your brain works and how it learns stuff is a fascinating subject but I haven't included it here for the same reason as why you don't get a book on electromagnetism when you buy a phone. It's simply not necessary. Besides which, I'm sure you've got enough to study without having to get into cognitive psychology as well. But if you really do want to find out more, you might like to read 'How We Learn' by Benedict Carey.

YOUR OWN TIPS

The tips I have included in this book are the ones that, for me, are the most important and the easiest to apply. But just because they work for me doesn't mean there aren't others that might work better for you.

To take this into account, here are a couple of blank pages for you to write down any other really useful tips you might have come across but keep forgetting. Trap them on these pages and apply them as often as you can.

FINAL EVALUATION

We started this little book by saying that learning is a skill, or if you prefer, a collection of techniques which when put together combine to help you study, remember and understand stuff better.

You might already have been aware of some of these 23 tips. Others you might already be applying in one form or another, while others might be relatively new tips for you.

Finally, it's time for a bit of honest self-assessment. How would you grade yourself on how well you're using each technique? The reason for doing this is simple. Knowing about a way of doing something is one thing, but actually putting it into practice is another.

So here is your opportunity to see what your current level of each technique is. Look at the following evaluation form and mark how good you are for each tip (The extra rows are to evaluate your own tips if you have any). By doing this, you will identify where there's room for improvement and think about what you could be doing differently to help yourself learn just a little bit better.

Once you've done it, the choice (and responsibility) is yours. You can carry on doing things exactly the same as before, or you can take the first steps along a new and exciting path. Which do you think it will be?

		☠	☹	😐	☺	🏆
1	Ownership					
2	Proactivity					
3	Resourcefulness					
4	Preparation					
5	Immediacy					
6	Little by little					
7	Environment					
8	Concentration					
9	Mistake acceptance					
10	Mistake leverage					
11	Planning					
12	Routines					
13	Rewards					
14	Flashcards					
15	Underlining					
16	Notetaking					
17	Illustrations					
18	Explaining					
19	Peer support					
20	Gamifying					
21	Practice					
22	Overlearning					
23	Reviewing					

How would you grade your learning skills?

WHAT NOW?

It's tempting to think there is a quick fix for learning. It would be great if you could learn Modern history simply by taking a little pink pill.

Unfortunately, it's not like that. None of the tips in this book is a little pink pill. None of them is going to improve your learning ability by a dramatic amount overnight.

Nevertheless, each one will improve your learning ability by a small amount. If you apply one tip for one week, the difference will be small—so small you'll hardly notice a difference at all.

If you apply all the tips over an academic year, all these small improvements will add up. They will reinforce each other, combining to become something formidable. You'll start to notice you're understanding stuff better, that your grades are steadily improving and you feel more confident about both your subjects and your capability as a student.

Of course, it's unlikely you will take on all of these tips. Some of them will be more appealing than others, while others simply won't apply to your situation or be possible due to your circumstance.

So, please, take these tips, pick the ones you feel match your needs the best and try them out for a month or two. Tweak them if you need to. Adjust them to fit the way you study. But don't expect miracles to happen straight away. Miracles do happen, but they need time.

What separates the successful students from the non-successful ones is knowing the best ways to study and to persevere with them right to the end.

Be patient and keep going.

APPENDIX: THE LEVELS OF LEARNING

Although it's not necessary for your studies, you might like to think for a moment about the levels of learning. Going from complete ignorance to Grand Master doesn't happen in one go. Like any worthwhile journey, it takes many steps. If we take ignorance as being at the bottom and mastery as being at the top, then the learning process can be thought of as a ladder with each rung being one of the steps.

For the purpose of this little book, it's enough to say there are five basic steps to learning.[8] They are Recognition, Recollection, Comprehension, Evaluation and Mastery.

The Levels of Learning

Recognition is the simplest. When you see a thing you've seen before, you recognise it. At the recognition level, if you don't have something to remind you such as having that thing in

---

8- If you're thinking about going into educational psychology one day, you'll discover there are a few more including Analysis, Synthesis, Application and Creation. But this is a simplified explanation and honestly, it's not worth bothering yourself about for now.

front of you, you struggle to remember it. You need some sort of prompt. You might recognise the page about hydrochloric acid of your chemistry book because you looked at it in class last month, but there's no way you could remember what's it's about without seeing it again or being given a clue.

Recollection is when you can remember stuff at will. You can recite names, dates, laws and formula without having to be given any sort of help at all. You can remember several facts about hydrochloric acid without having to look at the book or your notes. You might not understand much of it, but being able to remember those details whenever you want is now possible.

Comprehension is not only being able to recall information, it's understanding what that information means, how it fits together with other stuff and what you can do with it all. So if you're at the comprehension level, you know what hydrochloric acid is, its composition, characteristics and hopefully a few things it's useful for. Furthermore, you can explain all this using your own words, not just repeating the stuff you were able to remember at the previous level.

Evaluation is where you've learnt so much you can start to criticise what you've learnt about hydrochloric acid. Is the textbook right? Could the explanation be better? Are the details correct? What are the pros and cons of using hydrochloric acid? Is there any important information missing? At the Evaluation level, your circle of knowledge has increased well beyond the traditional limits of understanding.

Mastery is when you become the expert. You know pretty much everything there is to know. Not only can you evaluate, you can come up with your own stuff, too. You can create new thoughts, new ideas, new ways to do things and new ways to solve problems. You can make your own hydrochloric acid quicker and more efficiently than anyone else. You might even discover new types of hydrochloric acid or new uses for it. Once you get to this stage, you really do know that you've learnt it the best you can. But it will take you a while to do so.

As a rule of thumb, Secondary School education aims to get you to Comprehension level. Your time at College or University will get you to Evaluation level and if you want to become a Grand Master, think about doing a doctorate. But this is a very general rule of thumb. There are plenty of exceptions and I've come across people who've achieved mastery of their field of expertise without ever stepping foot in a place of higher education.

After all, learning stuff doesn't depend on teachers and buildings. It depends on how much you want to learn and how good your methods for learning it are.

Thanks

Thank you very much for taking the time to read this book. I hope it's been useful. If you've got this far, you're either a very dedicated reader, bored out of your skull or genuinely curious about who's helped me put this book together.

Therefore in addition to you, the reader, I'd also like to give a big thank you to the following: to my wife Olga for her patience and proofreading, to my publisher Gillian who believed in this project, to Benoît Corman who helped turn a good idea into a great one, to my lifelong study buddy Gary Dixon, to Sir Ken Robinson whose work in Education never ceases to inspire, Gemma López Jornet (from Jonqueres Institute) for taking the time to listen and talk, to Elisabet Sitges (Montserrat Secondary School) for volunteering to meet, Jo Johnson (CIC Cultural Institute) for her enthusiastic support, Salvador Rodriguez (Consorci d'Educació de Barcelona) for listening to me and all his useful information, to Tobias Rodrigues for his inspiring words and workshops, to John Firth (Kirkcudbright Academy) for his experience and hospitality, to Charlie Sardañes for his useful opinions and observations, to Julie Nash for her helpful support and to Martina Capallera Sais for her time and valuable feedback. I'd also like to mention my children, Sol and Alex along with their cousins Cadence, Chloè, George, Joe, Dan and Annie. I hope one day this can make a difference for them. Finally, I'd like to thank the teachers and students who've shared their opinions over the years and who unknowingly helped shape the destiny of these pages. Thank you to you all.

Biography

Author, speaker, business owner, company director, and playwright, Ian Gibbs was born in Sheffield, England, where his family was convinced that due to his shy, retiring nature he would never venture far from home.

After completing his degree in Theoretical Physics, Astronomy and Astrophysics in St. Andrews, Scotland, and his postgraduate diploma in Education in Cambridge, he decided he wanted a bit of adventure and went to work in Barcelona for a year (or maybe two) to teach English. One day he woke up to realise he's now been there for most of his life.

He now gives presentations and offers business coaching on learning and public speaking. When he's not coaching or speaking, he writes. He is the creator of 11 plays for children, one bilingual story book, the USSB model for improving personal productivity, and numerous personal development articles.

He has written three books to date: *The Sorites Principle: How to harness the power of perseverance, Learning a Language: How I managed it. How you can too,* and *23 Tips to Learn Stuff Better.*

He lives in the beautiful Collserola Natural Park overlooking Barcelona on the Mediterranean coast. He is married, has two children and a bouncy dog.

The Sorites Principle: How to harness the power of perseverance

Ian Gibbs

Everyone knows the stuff about 'a journey of a thousand miles begins with a single step' but few of us actually make the most of it. This is because it's misleading. The successful journey of a thousand miles begins with a lot of planning and preparation for those difficult times to come. It also involves learning how to cultivate a resilient perseverance that will keep you going when you start to confuse slow progress with no progress.

This book looks at how to apply the Sorites Principle (that the constant application of insignificant actions when coherently focussed will inevitably lead to dramatically significant results) and how to overcome the feelings of futility, procrastination and the inevitable lack of willpower.

Whether you want to lose weight, learn a new language, become a film director, write your first book or just want to keep your home clean and tidy, the Sorites Principle may be just what you need: a powerful unification of tips, tricks and techniques on how to achieve great things via small efforts.

So take your first step towards your life goals by reading this book and start achieving your dreams today.

If you'd like to download and print off some very practical and useful worksheets to help measure your progress, you can find them here:

http://www.guid-publications.com/soritesworksheets/201

Learning a Language: How I managed it. How you can, too.

Ian Gibbs

Usually, books about learning languages are written by enthusiasts who have learnt loads of languages. These amazing people are empowered to steam ahead due to their innate interest and pride with their subject.

In contrast, the author of this book is not a linguist. He doesn't wake up thinking about what language he can conquer today. He's perfectly satisfied with a tea and toast and to knock out 500 words in a language he feels more at home in.

Whereas in almost every other language learning circumstance, 'not being keen' is a disadvantage, with this book it has been of great importance.

This book is written by someone who, much like yourself, isn't a fanatic. He didn't write a thesis on the subject, he doesn't have a degree or even an 'A' level in any foreign language. His only qualification before writing this book was a CSE grade 4 in Spanish which, ironically, he's quite proud about. Nevertheless, by using the tricks and techniques in these pages, Ian learnt to speak a new language in less than six months.

Uniquely, this is a book about language learning written for non-linguists by a non-linguist. He hopes you notice, appreciate and enjoy the difference.

23 Tips to Get Higher Grades

Ian Gibbs

Learning stuff better is important. Getting stuff off the page and into your head is what education is all about, isn't it?

But what's the point if you go and make a mess of it all in your exams?

After all, knowing your stuff is one thing but, unfortunately, knowing how to ace an exam is another.

We all know of too many cases where students failed to get the grade they deserved because they were paralysed with nerves, or ran out of time, or didn't even read the question correctly.

What's even more frustrating for them is that these mistakes could have been so easily avoided. How? Well, you're going to have to wait. 23 Tips to Get Better Grades will be out soon with the most practical, helpful, and effective tips to help you calm your nerves, clear your head, answer the right questions in the right way, and get the grade you truly deserve.

Let's hope it will be soon enough!

For more of our books, visit: http://www.guid-publications.com